PATHAN

THE KING OF TRIBES

GOLU KUMAR

This incident has been written by a British soldier, this book is not meant to show anyone's caste as big or small, this book is not meant to be read-only.

Contents

CHAPTER ONE

PATHAN THE KING OF TRIBES

The whole of the country lying immediately to the west of Punjab, and between it and the kingdom of Afghanistan, is held by the two great nations of Pathan and Baluch, the former lying to the north and the latter to the south of a line drawn from the western face of the Suleiman Mountains opposite Dera Ghazi Khan, almost due west to Quetta. The land, then, of the Pathans may be said to comprise the regions of the Surfed Koh and the Suleiman and adjacent mountains with their numerous offshoots; and their territory may be considered roughly to be enclosed by the River Indus on the east, by Afghanistan on the west, Baluchistan on the south, and the north by Kashmir and the Kunar River—a veritable _tangle_ of brown hills. "It is a long strip of the unutterably rugged country; stony barren heights, deep abrupt valleys seamed by occasional torrents; the farms represented by a patch of corn on a hillside or a scrap of cultivation on a narrow strip of alluvial soil alongside a mountain stream. No highways, save those made by us; the village roads—mere tracks straggling over hills and among the roughest ravines—are always difficult and often dangerous. The dwelling places, fortified towers or caves among the hills." The Pathan territories occupy many thousand square miles of the mountainous country through which flow the Gomal, the Kurram, the Zhob, the Kabul, and other smaller rivers with their tributaries, the principal tributaries of the Kabul River being the Chitral, the Bara, the Swat, and the Kalpani. The rainfall in this region is scanty and uncertain, and agriculture can only properly be carried on in those tracts watered by these rivers. The language of the Pathan is called Pushtu or Pukhtu, according as it is the softer Kandahari dialect or the hard guttural speech of the Peshawar Valley, the line which separates the two is the northern boundary of the Khattak tract in Kohat and the south-east corner of the Peshawar District. It is only since the fourteenth century that Pushtu has attained the dignity of a written language. And what of the men who speak it? What is a Pathan?

[Sidenote: Pathan Descent]

In India all Pushtu-speaking people come under this designation—a corruption of the word "Pukhtun"—the term is frequently used to denote equally the Pathan proper, the Afghan, the Tajik, the Hazara, and the Ghilzai; but, strictly speaking, the title does not apply to any of the four last, who, though related to the true Pathan by historical, geographical and ethnological association, are none the less distinct peoples. There is a great conflict of opinion as to the original stock from which the Pathans have sprung—the traditions of the people themselves are conflicting, vague, and misleading, but the Pathans believe that they are descended from Saul, the first King of the Jews. They speak of themselves as "Beni Israel," the children of Israel and the greybeards of the Pathan tribes are fond of tracing their story back to Ibrahim, Isak, and Yakub. However far-fetched and mainly traditionary the connection may be, there is, as discussed by Bellew, a savor of Israelitish custom and often remarkable similarity of the name still surviving—Amazites, Moabites, and Hittites live again in Amazai, Muhibwal, and Hotiwal, to be found on Mount Morah, the hill Pehor, and the plain of Galilee (Jalala); there is the valley of Sedum; the observance of the "Passover," offering sin and thank offerings, or driving off the scapegoat laden with the sins of the people—with many other religious and social observances which are Jewish rather than Islamic in their origin. It would seem that the Pathan race is closely allied to the Afghans on the one side, and, though perhaps not so closely, to certain tribes of Aryan Indians on the other. (The language is a mixture of partly Persian, partly Indian—Prakrit—origin.) The Pathan may be indeed described as an Indian Afghan, and the probabilities are that he represents an earlier eastern emigration of certain sections of the same tribes as having given birth to the Afghan, and from this point of view, the Pathan and the Afghan are by origin the same. Whatever view is correct, there can be no doubt that the Pathan differs from the Afghan in the possession of certain Indian affinities not present in the other. Whether these are due to an admixture of Indian blood, or whether they are merely the result of close and prolonged political and social contact with India, is a matter of no very particular importance. Ibbetson favors the theory that the Pathans are in the main a race of Indian extraction, that is, that the Pathan stock is decidedly Indian despite the admixture of foreign blood. According to him, the true Pathans are the modern representatives of an Aryan Indian race called Herodotus the Pactiyae, which gave birth to many of the tribes represented today in and on the borders of the Peshawar Valley. According to this view, the Pathans proper are those

Pathan tribes that have a decidedly Pactiyan stock, in which the preponderating racial element is Indian; while the mixed Pactiyan and foreign tribes in which the stock is not Indian, but Afghan, Turk, or Scythian, as the case may be, are Pathan by their Pactiyan blood, as well as by their geographical location, association, customs and language. But that the stock is in the main Afghan rather than Indian, seems borne out by the fact that from the earliest times of which historical records exist, we find the Pathan ever arrayed against and despising the Indian—evincing an antagonism which is not merely practical and political, but one of ideas and sentiment. On the other hand, although the Pathan tribes have had constant and bloody feuds with the Afghans, in their brief periods of peace they display a marked similarity of sentiment, ideals, and aims, while the mental characteristics of the Pathan also approximate much more closely to the Afghan than to those of any purely Indian tribe. Of the other races and tribes to which the term Pathan is loosely applied, the _Ghilzais_ are a race of mixed Turkish and Persian descent, which has now become assimilated with the Afghans by sentiment and association. The _Tajiks_, another to which the term Pathan is applied, are of pure Persian origin and are believed to be the remnants of certain Persian tribes who once inhabited Afghanistan before the advent of the Afghans by whom they were subdued. The Tajiks still retain their Persian speech. The _Hazaras_ are Persian-speaking Tartars who have long settled among the Afghans, but who hold among them a subordinate and dependent position.

[Sidenote: Character]

The character of the Pathan is a favorite theme of disparagement amongst the frontier officials of the last half-century and more. In 1855, Mr. Temple, then Secretary to the Chief Commissioner of Punjab, wrote thus of them: "Now these tribes are savages—noble savages perhaps—and not without some tincture of virtue and generosity, but still absolutely barbarians nevertheless... They have nominally a religion, but Muhammadanism, as understood by them, is no better, or perhaps is worse, than the creeds of the wildest race on earth. In their eyes, the one great commandment is blood for blood, and fire and sword for all infidels... They are superstitious and priest-ridden. But the priests are as ignorant as they are bigoted, and use their influence simply for preaching crusades against unbelievers and inculcate the doctrine of rapine and bloodshed against the defenseless people of the plain... They are a sensual race. They are very avaricious; for gold, they will do almost anything, except betray a guest. They are thievish and predatory to the last degree. The Pathan's mother offers prayers that her son may be a successful robber. They are utterly faithless in public engagements; it would never even occur to their minds that an oath on the Koran was binding, if against their interests... They are fierce and bloodthirsty ... they are perpetually at war with each other. Every tribe and section of a tribe has its internecine wars, every family its hereditary blood feuds, and every individual his foes. There is hardly a man whose hands are unstained. Every person counts up his murders. Each tribe has a debtor and creditor account with its neighbors, life for life... They consider retaliation and revenge to be the strongest of all obligations. They possess gallantry and courage themselves and admire such qualities in others... To their minds hospitality is the first of virtues. Any person who can make his way into their dwellings will not only be safe but will be kindly received. But as soon as he has left the roof of his entertainer he may be robbed and killed."

[Sidenote: Code of Honour]

Mr. Ibbetson wrote of the Pathan in 1881: “The true Pathan is perhaps the most barbaric of all the races with which we are brought into contact in Punjab... He is bloodthirsty, cruel, and vindictive in the highest degree; he does not know what truth or faith is, insomuch that the saying _Afghan be iman_ (_i.e._ an Afghan is without a conscience) has passed into a proverb among his neighbors; and though he is not without the courage of a sort, and is often curiously reckless of his life, he would scorn to face an enemy whom he could stab from behind, or to meet him on equal terms if it were possible to take advantage of him, however meanly. It is easy to convict him out of his mouth; here are some of his proverbs: ‘a Pathan’s enmity smolders like a dung fire’; ‘a cousin’s tooth breaks upon a cousin’;

[1] ‘keep a cousin poor but use him’; ‘when he is little play with him; when he is grown up he is a cousin, fight him’; ‘speak good words to an enemy very softly; gradually destroy him root and branch.’ At the same time, he has a code of honor that he strictly observes, which he quotes with pride under the name of _Pukhtunwali_. It imposes on him three chief obligations—_Nanawatai_, or the right of asylum, which compels him to shelter and protect even an enemy who comes as a suppliant; _Badal_, or the necessity for revenge by retaliation; and _Mailmastai_, or openhanded hospitality to all who may demand it. And of these three perhaps the last is the greatest. And there is a charm about him, especially about the leading men, which almost makes one forget his treacherous nature. As the proverb says—‘the Pathan is one moment a saint, and the next a devil.’ For centuries he has been, on our frontier at least, subject to no man. He leads a wild, free, active life in the rugged fastnesses of his mountains; and there is an air

of masculine independence about him which is refreshing in a country like India. He is a bigot of the most fanatical type, exceedingly proud and extraordinarily superstitious." Holdich says of the Pathan that "he will shoot his relations just as soon as the relations of his enemy—possibly sooner—and he will shoot them from behind. Yet the individual Pathan may be trusted to be true to his salt and his engagements." Of one Pathan tribe Macgregor said that "there is no doubt, like other Pathans, they would not shrink from any falsehood, however atrocious, to gain an end. Money could buy their services for the foulest deed; the cruelty of the most revolting kind would mark their actions to a wounded or helpless foe, as much as cowardice would stamp them against determined resistance." While Mr. Elsmie has spoken as follows of his five years' experience as a Commissioner and Judge among the Pathans of the Peshawar border: "Crime of the worst conceivable kind is a matter of almost daily occurrence; murder in all its phases, unblushing assassination in broad daylight before a crowd of witnesses; the carefully planned secret murder of the sleeping victim at dead of night, murder by robbers, by rioters, by poisoners, by boys, and by women sword in hand. Blood always crying for blood, revenge looked upon as a virtue, the heritage of retribution passed on as a solemn duty from father to son. It would seem that the spirit of murder is latent in the heart of nearly every man in the valley." But, on the other hand, Oliver tells us in _Across the Border_, that the Pathan has sometimes been condemned in what appear too sweeping terms, and that "there is a sort of charm about the better sort that inclines many people to forget his treacherous nature, and even his 'vice is sometimes by action dignified.'"

[Sidenote: A Juster Judgment]

Probably what Lieut. Enriquez says about these tribesmen in his _Pathan Borderland_ describes them with, on the whole, more justice, if less vehemence, than have some of those other writers from whom quotations have here been made. "The Pathan," he says, "is not so black as he is painted. It should not be overlooked that most of the tribes have only been established three hundred years in their present territories and that their habits are not much worse than were those of the various English tribes during the first few centuries after their final settlement. The conditions of a feudal system, under which each baron lived in his castle, and waged constant war with his neighbors over disputes relating to land and women, are simply being repeated across our border. For stories of gross treachery, or cold-blooded murder and inter-family strife, we have only to turn back the pages of our history book. It seems quite unfair to judge the Pathan according to twentieth-century standards. For him, it is still the tenth century. Moreover, it is ungenerous to assert that there are not many noble exceptions amongst them... When you meet a Pathan, you meet a man like yourself... He will never allow you to abuse him but makes up for it amply by never making you wish to do so. There is perhaps no native of India who is less irritating to our nerves, and his ideas of tact seem to run on quite the same lines as our own... He takes his independence for granted, and very seldom parades it in the garb of rudeness." Take him for all in all, there is in the Pathan much to like, a good deal to respect, and much to detest. He is very susceptible to the personal influence of Englishmen who are strong, resolute, and fearless—men of the type of Nicholson, Abbott, Cavagnari, Battye, and many others. In our service, he has usually been a loyal and devoted sepoy, and no better instance of the loyalty of the Pathan soldier can be given than is furnished by that of the small body of Khyber Rifles in 1897, who, as Holdich has told us, "maintained British honor in the Khyber, while 9,500 British troops about the Peshawar frontier looked on."

[Sidenote: Blood feuds]

The Pathan enlists freely into our service—there are at the present moment something like eleven thousand Pathans in the Indian Army, and probably the recruiting among the tribesmen was never brisker than during the few months immediately following the close of the operations in Tirah of 1897–98—and he will march anywhere and fight anyone against whom he may be led. Over and over again Pathans fought in our ranks against their fellow tribesmen and their own homes. Not only against fathers and brothers but even against the still more potent religious appeals from the local Ghazis. One thing, however, the Pathan recruit does not give up, "but brings with him to his regiment, keeps through his service, must have leave to look after, will resign promotion to gratify, and looks forward to retiring to thoroughly enjoy—and that is—his cherished feud." If he has not got one when he joins, he may inherit one which may become just as binding, though it concerns people he has not seen for years, and hardly knew when he left home. In India the white man wants to leave to get married, he is sick, he needs a change, or to avoid a bad station—for the Pathan soldier there is only one class of "urgent private affairs," but for this, he must have left. Everyone knows for what purpose he goes; it is the only reason when the refusal of leave would justify desertion. In many of the Punjab regiments which recruit Pathans there are cases of trans-frontier soldiers who will serve together in all amity for years, but between whom is so bitter a feud that they must take their furlough at different times, since, if they went together, not all would come back. As to the personal appearance of "the raw material," here is a picture is drawn from life by Oliver: "The style of the Tribesman is a little after the manner of Rob Roy—'my foot is on my native heath,' and 'am I not a Pathan'? Even when he leaves his native heath behind, he takes his manners with him. He will come down, a stalwart, manly-looking ruffian, with frank and open manners, rather Jewish features, long hair plentifully oiled under a high turban, with a loose tunic, blue for choice—the better to hide the dirt—worn very long, baggy drawers, a _lungi_ or sash across his shoulders, grass sandals, a sheepskin coat with the hair inside, thickly populated, a long heavy knife, and a rifle, if he is allowed to carry either. He is certain to be filthy and he may be ragged, but he will saunter into a Viceregal _durbar_ as proud as Lucifer, and with an air of unconcern a diplomatist might envy."

[Sidenote: Leaders]

The Pathan tribes are partly agriculturists and partly nomads, but their migrations are on a small and restricted scale, being no more than annual moves within their limits from one grazing ground to another, or from their homes among the hills to the warmer and lower valleys. Beyond and upon our frontier the Pathans live in fortified villages, to which are attached stone towers in commanding positions serving as watchtowers and places of refuge for the inhabitants. A large number of the men of each tribe obtain their livelihood as petty merchants or traders, carrying goods in caravans between India, Afghanistan, and Central Asia. These wandering traders are called _Powindahs_, a term derived from the Persian word _Parwindah_, which signifies a bale of goods. The villages are divided into several distinct allotments of sub-divisions called _Kandis_, according to the number of the sub-divisions of the tribe residing in it. Thus in each village, each group of families that goes to form a _Khel_or clan, has its own Kandi, at the head of which is a _Malik_, who acts as its judge, manager, or an administrator. In each Kandi, again, there is a _Jumaat_, or mosque, under a _Mullah_, or priest, and an assembly room called _hujra_, where the residents meet to discuss their affairs, and where visitors and travelers are sheltered. At the head of each clan is a chief styled _Khan_, to whom the _Maliks_ are subordinate, but the tribesmen being intensely independent and impatient of control, it is not surprising that neither Maliks nor Khans enjoy any real power. They may be said indeed to possess influence rather than power. All matters of general tribal interest are settled by the decision of a _jirgah_ or council of Maliks and in this, the real controlling authority resides, the Khan, or tribal chief, merely acting as president of the tribal jirga, as their leader in a time of war, and during peace as their accredited agent for inter-tribal communication. But among the Pathans, there can be very little ordered government, and the several clans decide their disputes independently of any central controlling authority. The office of Malik and Khan is usually hereditary, but by no means always. It is not very uncommon for families of one tribe or clan to quarrel with their brethren and leave their tribe, to claim the protection of a neighboring one. They then become _hamsayas_, or "dwellers beneath the shade," and secure protection in return for obedience. With the Pathans, the action of this custom is chiefly confined to traders, menials, and other dependents of foreign extraction, who are protected by, but not received into, the tribe. The great majority of the

Pathan tribes are Sunni[2] Muhammadans of a bigoted sort, the exception being the Turis and some of the Bangash and Orakzai clansmen, who are Shiahs. Of the different dignitaries of the Pathan Church, there is no occasion here to speak further than to remark that the Mullah, to whom allusion has already been made, is the ordinary, hard-working parish priest, whose duties are to attend to the services of the Church, teach the creed, and look after the schools. He is the most important factor in Pathan's life and his influence is enormous, despite the fact, as Dr. Pennell points out, "that there is no priesthood in Islam," and that according to its tenets, there is no act of worship and no religious rite which may not, in the absence of a Mullah, be equally well performed by any pious layman. Since, however, "knowledge has been almost limited to the priestly class, it is only natural that in a village, where the Mullahs are almost the only men who can lay claim to anything more than the most rudimentary learning, they should have the people of the village entirely in their control." The general security in which the Mullah lives is the best possible evidence of the deference accorded to his office. "He is almost the only man," says Oliver, "whose life is sacred from the casual bullet or the hasty knife, for whose blood the Pathan tariff does not provide a rate." His flock is generally ignorant of everything connected with the Muhammadan religion beyond its most elementary doctrines. In matters of faith, the Pathans confine themselves to the belief that there is a God, a prophet, a resurrection, and a day of judgment. They know there is a Koran, but are probably wholly ignorant of its contents. Their practice is un-Islamic. Though they repeat every day that there is one God only who is worthy of worship, they almost invariably prefer to worship some saint or tomb.

Indeed, superstition is a more appropriate term for the ordinary belief of the people than the name of religion.

[Sidenote: Gar and Samil]

Since mention has above been made of the religious divisions of the tribesmen, I may perhaps briefly allude to their political factions, since reports from beyond the border make frequent mention of the feuds of Gar and Samil. In the fourteenth century a chief of the Bangash tribe, Ismail by name, had two sons, Gar and Samil, whose quarrels led to the tribe being split up into the two great factions which still exist under these names. Bangash or Bankash means "root-destroyer," and this was adopted or bestowed as the tribal name because of the enmity aroused between the rival factions. The distinction then established remains, and affects almost all the surrounding tribes; and since some Sunnis by religion are Samil in politics, and some Shiahs are Gar, while sometimes both cases are reversed, it may easily be realized how prolific are the causes for private quarrels and tribal feuds beyond the Bloody Border. Of so turbulent a race what Temple said about them in 1855 might with almost equal truth have been repeated of them annually up to the present time: "They have kept up old quarrels, or picked new ones with our subjects in the plains and valleys near the frontier; they have descended from the hills and fought these battles out in our territory; they have plundered and burnt our villages and slain our subjects; they have committed minor robberies and isolated murders without number; they have often levied blackmail from our villages; they have intrigued with the disaffected everywhere and tempted our loyal subjects to rebel, and they have for ages regarded the plain as their preserve and its inhabitants as their game. When inclined for the cruel sport they sally forth to rob and murder and occasionally take prisoners into captivity for ransom. They have fired upon our troops, and even killed our officers in our territories. They have given asylum to every malcontent or proclaimed criminal who can escape from British justice. They traverse at will our territories, enter our villages, trade-in our markets; but few British subjects, and no servant of the British Government, would dare to enter their country on any account whatever." Since the 400 miles of our borderland, comprised in the stretch from Buner on the right to Waziristan on the left, is, as computed by the Commander-in-Chief in India in 1897, inhabited by 200,000 first-rate fighting men, of the quarrelsome character above described—every man at all times ready and eager for blood-letting—it would be as well now to recount the measures which the Government of India adopts for their restraint; to state the composition and general distribution of the instruments using which the peace of the frontier is more or less preserved, and to note how offenses committed by independent tribes beyond the border are punished.

[Sidenote: Defence of the Frontier]

For the defense of the border, and to prevent the incursion of armed robbers, the system generally followed—with some recent modifications—has been the maintenance of a line of fortified posts along the frontier, garrisoned by regulars and militia. In the year 1884 there were fifty-four such posts situated in the Hazara, Yusafzai, Kohat, Bannu, Dera Ismail Khan, Dera Ghazi Khan, and Rajanpur districts, and of these sixteen were held by the Punjab Frontier Force, twenty-six by militia, and the remainder by combined parties of both militia and regulars. In those days the Punjab Frontier Force was generally responsible—a responsibility which endured until 1903—for the military defense of the frontier, except for the Peshawar district. The force was approximately 15,000 strong and consisted of four regiments of cavalry, the Guides (cavalry and infantry), four mountain batteries, one garrison battery, and eleven infantry battalions, the whole commanded by a Brigadier-General. At that time it was immediately under the orders of the Lieutenant-Governor of Punjab, but it was a few years later placed under the Commander-in-Chief in India. With the gradual extension of the frontier and the general forward movement made within recent years, it became apparent that the Punjab Frontier Force could no longer remain a local and also a border force, and that in any comprehensive scheme of frontier defense other regiments of the Indian army must take their share. In 1903, then, the Punjab Frontier Force was abolished. Under Lord Curzon's rule in India, a change was inaugurated in the system of frontier defense. Regular troops have been gradually withdrawn, as far as possible, from advanced trans-frontier positions, and have been concentrated in large centers within easy reach. Their places on the border have been taken by various corps of militia, military police, and levies raised locally; communications have been improved; strategic railways have crept further forward; another bridge has been thrown across the Indus; and the frontier is now defended by the Peshawar and Quetta divisions and the Kohat, Derajat and Bannu brigades, moveable columns being held always ready to move out at a moment's notice from Peshawar, Kohat, Bannu, and Dera Ismail Khan. The general sphere of action prescribed for each of these columns is as under Peshawar Column, The Khyber, and the Malakand. Kohat Column, The Kurram. Bannu Column,

The Tochi. Dera Ismail Khan Column, Waziristan. It remains to note how offenses committed by independent tribes across the border are punished. The most simple way of dealing with a refractory tribe, and in many cases the most effectual, is to inflict a fine and demand compensation for plundered property or lives lost. When the tribe is dependent upon trade with British territory, or when a portion resides within British limits or is easily accessible from the plains to an attack by a military force, the demand for payment of fine or compensation is generally acceded to, and, being paid, the tribe is again received into favor. Should the demand be refused, hostages are demanded, or members of the tribe and their property found within British territory are seized, until the compensation and fine are paid. Against some tribes, as in the case of the Afridis of the Kohat Pass in 1876–77, a blockade is an effective measure of punishment. It can, however, only be employed against such tribes as trade with British territory, and, while it lasts, any member of the offending tribe found within our border is at once seized and detained. This means of punishment has often been found effectual, and if effectual, it is preferable to a military expedition, which often leaves behind it bitter memories of the destruction of property and loss of life. Last, a measure of punishment comes to the military expedition, which is only resorted to in exceptional circumstances, and when every other means of coercing a hostile tribe has failed.

[Sidenote: Coercive Measures]

The necessity, in certain circumstances, for military expeditions has been admitted by the civil authorities of Punjab in the following statement made in 1864 by Mr. Davies, Secretary to the Punjab Government: "The despatch of an expedition into the hills is always like a judicial act. It is the delivery of a sentence and the infliction of punishment for international offenses. It is, as a rule, not in the assertion of any disputed right, or in ultimate arbitration of any contested claim of its own, that the British Government resolves on such measures, but simply as the only means by which retribution can be obtained for acknowledged crimes by its neighbors, and by which justice can be satisfied or future outrages prevented. In the extreme cases in which expeditions are unavoidable, they are analogous to legal penalties for civil crime—evils in themselves inevitable from deficiencies of preventive police but redeemed by their deterrent effects. Considerations of expense, of military risk, of possible losses, of incurring antagonism and combination against us on the part of the tribes, all weigh heavily against expeditions; and to set them aside, there must be an irresistible obligation to protect and to vindicate the outraged rights of subjects whom we debar from the revenge and retaliation they formerly practiced." At the present moment rather over 9000 Pathans are serving in our militias, border military police, and levies, while considerably more than 10,000 are in the ranks of the regular regiments of the Indian army; a certain number, too, is serving in the forces maintained by native chiefs. Considering the readiness with which the Pathan accepts military service, it cannot be said that these numbers are high, but the fact would seem to be that while some tribes are supplying us with more recruits than they can well afford, others have scarcely been drawn upon at all, and many races along the Pathan borderland remain still altogether unexploited.

[Sidenote: The N.W.F. Province]

[3]The North-West Frontier Province is, except for Behar, Chota Nagpur, and Orissa, the youngest of the provinces into which British India is divided, while in respect of population and extent of the territory administered according to British law, it is also the smallest. It lies between the 31st and 36th degrees of latitude and the 69th and 74th degrees of longitude; its total length, as the crow flies, is over 400 miles, its average breadth is from 100 to 150 miles, the total area comprised within its limits being roughly 38,000 square miles. Only 13,000 square miles, however, are under full British law and administration, and 25,000 square miles are occupied by tribes who are under British political control, but who maintain their internal or municipal independence. The British territory part of the province is divided into the five districts of Hazara, Peshawar, Kohat, Bannu, and Dera Ismail Khan, whose western boundary, known as the administrative border, is a sinuous line extending for some 600 miles. On the other side of this administrative or inner provincial border dwell the municipally independent tribes who are under the political control of the Chief Commissioner, a control which he exercises with the aid of the officers in charge of the political agencies, viz. Swat, Dir and Chitral, the Khyber, the Kurram, and Northern, and Southern Waziristan. These agencies have been described as the tentacles of civilized order, stretching into a mass of barbarism and savagery; and the remainder of the space beyond the administrative border and as far as the "Durand Line" or "the outer provincial border," separating the British and Afghan spheres of influence, is occupied by the independent tribes. The length of this outer border cannot be less than 800 miles. The population of the five British districts is about 2,200,000, and of the outer portion of the

province probably a million and a half. After the border war of 1897 a narrow-gauge line was laid from Nowshera, on the Kabul River, to the foot of the Malakand; constructed in the first instance for military reasons, it rapidly developed into an important artery of commerce, justifying its conversion from a narrow to a broad gauge. Another railway which, in 1897, stopped on the left bank of the Indus at Kushalgarh, now crosses the Indus by a bridge and has been extended via Kohat and Hangu to Thal, at the southern end of the Kurram Valley. A third line to the base of the hills is under construction; it will be taken over the Indus at Kalabagh and carried to Bannu. When the Thal railway has been extended to the head of the Kurram Valley; when a short line has been constructed in the Hazara district; and when a lateral branch has been provided from Bannu to Tank and Dera Ismail Khan, the province will be fairly well equipped with railways of a distinct commercial and strategic value.

[Sidenote: Frontier Policy]

A perusal of the chapters which follow will probably make it apparent that the general policy of the Government of India regarding the frontier tribes is, and has been—as well described by a former Chief Commissioner of the North-West Frontier Province—"a forward one only when necessity compels, and stationary where circumstances permit."

9 798886 678437

Printed by Libri Plureos GmbH in Hamburg,
Germany